W9-CGQ-059

Sweet Specialities
from **Alsace**

...vours of yesterday and today

by

Gérard FRITSCH

& Guy ZEISSLOFF

Photos by

Frédérique CLEMENT

I. D. L'Édition

Contents

Desserts

Cupcakes

Recipes

Gâteau à la cannelle
Cinnamon cake or Zimmetkuche

Preparation : 30 min
Cooking : 30-35 min

Ingredients for one cinnamon cake weighing 500 to 600 g

For the dough

- *250 g flour*
- *40 g caster sugar*
- *5 g table salt*
- *1 egg*
- *10 g yeast*
- *90 g milk*
- *70 g butter*

Other ingredients
- *100 g thick crème fraîche*
- *100 g caster sugar*
- *10 g cinnamon*
- *20 g butter*

In the food mixer bowl or a large salad bowl, mix the flour, the sugar, the salt, the yeast, the egg and the milk.

Knead the dough by hand or with the kneading hook in the food mixer.

When the dough is smooth, add the softened butter.

Mix the dough until it is again smooth and evenly mixed.

Put the dough to one side, cover it with Clingfilm and allow it to double in volume in a warm place away from draughts.

When the dough has risen sufficiently, turn it out onto a floured work surface.

Flatten the dough with your hands and then fold the edges into the centre to form a ball.

Place the dough on a buttered oven tray and leave it to rise again away from draughts.

When the dough has doubled in volume, carefully spread the thick cream on the top.

Mix the caster sugar and the powdered cinnamon.

Liberally sprinkle the dough with the cinnamon sugar.

With your finger, makes holes in the dough at regular intervals.

Put a small knob of butter in each hole.

Bake in a preheated oven at 180°C.

It will take 30 to 35 minutes to cook.

Gâteau de santé
Health cake or Gesundheitskuchen

Preparation : 20 min
Cooking : 45-55 min

Ingredients

- *150 g butter*
- *225 g caster sugar*
- *3 eggs*
- *150 g milk*
- *300 g flour*
- *1 sachet of vanilla sugar or the zest of one lemon*
- *1 sachet of baking powder*

Other ingredients

- *Butter*
- *Flour*

Sift the flour and the baking powder.

Soften the butter in a salad bowl without allowing it to melt.

Whisk the butter, the sugar and the vanilla sugar together.

Add the eggs and carefully mix the preparation with a whisk.

With a spatula, incorporate the flour sifted with the baking powder.

Finish the preparation by adding the milk.

When the mixture is smooth, pour it into a buttered, floured cake tin.

Bake in a preheated oven at 180°C for around 45 to 55 min.

Kougelhopf

Preparation : 30 min
Cooking : 40-45 min

Ingredients for a mould around 25 cm in diameter

- 375 g flour
- 60 g caster sugar
- 7 g table salt
- 2 eggs
- 15 g yeast
- 115 g milk
- 90 g butter
- 20 g Alsatian kirsch
- 115 g sultanas
- 80 g whole almonds

Advice and special tips

It is best to use a traditional Kougelhopf mould in earthenware; even though it is more fragile, it is the reason for the special taste of the Kougelhopf.

*If you do not have any sultanas macerated in advance:
Put the sultanas in a bowl with rum or kirsch;
Cover the bowl with Clingfilm;
Put the bowl in the microwave for 2 minutes; And allow to cool before using the sultanas.*

The day before, macerate the sultanas in the kirsch.

In the food mixer bowl or a salad bowl, mix the flour, the eggs, the milk, the salt, the sugar and the yeast.

Knead the dough by hand or with the kneading hook in the food mixer.

When the dough is smooth and shiny, add the softened butter at room temperature.

Mix your dough again and, when it is evenly mixed, gently incorporate the macerated sultanas.

Put the dough to one side in a salad bowl and cover with Clingfilm or a clean cloth.

Allow the dough to double in volume in a warm place away from draughts.

Take a Kougelhopf mould 25 centimetres in diameter and liberally butter the sides of the mould.

Soak the almonds in a bowl of cold water and put one almond in the bottom of each groove in your Kougelhopf mould.

Turn out the Kougelhopf dough onto a lightly floured work surface.

Flatten the dough and fold the edges into the centre of your piece of dough until you obtain a ball.

Turn the ball over and, using your thumb, make a hole in the middle of the dough.

Place the dough in the mould and allow it to rise in a warm place away from draughts.

Bake the Kougelhopf in a preheated oven at 180°C once the dough has reached the top of the mould.

Cooking takes around 40 to 45 min depending on your oven.

Streussel

Preparation : 30 min
Cooking : 30-35 min

*Ingredients for one Streussel
weighing 500 to 600 g*

For the dough
- *250 g flour*
- *40 g caster sugar*
- *5 g table salt*
- *1 egg*
- *10 g yeast*
- *80 g milk*
- *60 g butter*

For the Streussel
- *100 g flour*
- *70 g butter*
- *70 g sugar*
- *1 teaspoon cinnamon (optional)*

Other ingredients
- *1 egg for the egg wash glaze*
- *A knob of butter*
- *Icing sugar*

For the dough

In the food mixer bowl or a large salad bowl, mix the flour, the sugar, the salt, the yeast, the egg and the milk.

Knead the dough by hand or with the kneading hook in the food mixer.

When the dough is smooth, add the softened butter.

Mix the dough until it is again smooth and evenly mixed.

Put the dough to one side, cover it with Clingfilm and allow it to double in volume in a warm place away from draughts.

For the Streussel

While this is happening, mix the flour, the sugar, the diced butter and the cinnamon in a bowl.

Knead the mixture by rubbing the ingredients between your hands to obtain little lumps of dough.

Put the Streussel in the fridge.

Butter a round mould or a 25-centimetre tart tin.

When the dough has risen sufficiently, turn it out onto a floured work surface.

Flatten the dough with your hands and then fold the edges into the centre to form a ball.

Roll out the ball to the size of your mould with a rolling pin.

Put the dough in the mould and leave it to rise again away from draughts.

When the dough has doubled in volume, brush it with the egg wash.

Crumble the Streussel over the dough and bake in a preheated oven at 180°C.

It will take 30 to 35 minutes to cook.

Take out of the mould and leave to cool on a rack.

Tarte à la rhubarbe meringuée
Rhubarb meringue tart

Preparation : 30 min
Cooking : 45-50 min

Prepare the tart pastry and leave it to rest in the fridge for 30 min.

Peel the rhubarb and cut it into 1 cm pieces.

Butter a 28-cm tart tin.

Roll out the pastry and put it in the tart tin. Sprinkle the bottom of the tart with the breadcrumbs.

Lay the pieces of rhubarb in the bottom of the tart.

Bake the tart in a preheated oven at 200°C.

For the tart custard

Whisk the egg and the sugar in a salad bowl until light and frothy.

Add the corn flour, mix and finish the custard by adding the milk or cream.

Bake the tart for around 20 to 25 min and pour the custard over your tart.

Put the tart back into the oven for around 25 to 35 min depending on the oven.

When cooked, take the tart out of its tin and put on a rack.

For the meringue

Whisk the egg whites with the caster sugar until stiff.

Add the icing sugar using a spatula.

Fill a piping bag fitted with a fluted 10-mm nozzle.

Pipe the meringue on to the tart and put back into the oven for around 10 min.

When the meringue starts to colour slightly, take the tart out of the oven and leave it to cool on a rack.

Ingredients for a tart tin with a diameter of around 28 cm

• *450 g short crust pastry (see recipe for apple tart page 78)*
• *700 g rhubarb*
• *50 g breadcrumbs*

For the tart custard
• *1 egg*
• *50 g sugar*
• *20 g corn flour*
• *100 g milk or crème fraîche*

For the meringue
• *3 egg whites*
• *100 g caster sugar*
• *100 g icing sugar*

Advice and tips

Mix the cut rhubarb with 100 g of icing sugar and leave it to release its water for around 2 hours. Drain the rhubarb before using.

If you do not wish to cover the tart with meringue, sprinkle it with caster sugar.

Tarte au fromage blanc
Cheesecake or KasKuche

Preparation : 20 min
Cooking : 1 hour

*Ingredients for one ring 20 cm
in diameter and 6 cm in height*

* *250 g crumbly short crust pastry
(see recipe page 78)*
* *300 g fromage blanc with 0% fat*
* *4 egg yolks*
* *Grated zest of ½ a lemon (optional)*
* *40 g corn flour*
* *4 egg whites*
* *140 g caster sugar*

Other ingredients and equipment
* *1 ring 6 cm in height*
* *30 g raisins macerated in rum*
* *1 tbsp icing sugar*

Prepare the crumbly short crust pastry and leave it to rest in the fridge. Butter the ring.

Roll out the pastry to a thickness of 4 mm and place it on an oven tray covered with greaseproof paper.

Press the ring into the pastry and remove the excess. Sprinkle the bottom with raisins.

For the fromage blanc mixture

Whisk the fromage blanc, the egg yolks, the lemon zest and the corn flour.

Using an electric whisk, beat the eggs with the sugar until stiff.

Carefully incorporate the beaten egg whites into the first mixture.

Pour the fromage blanc mixture into the ring and even it out.

Bake in a preheated oven at 160°C for around 60 min.

When your cheesecake is cooked, leave it to cool down and then turn it out on to a rack.

When completely cold, turn the cheesecake over and sprinkle the edges of the cheesecake with a little icing sugar.

Tarte aux cerises
Cherry tart or KirscheKuche

Preparation : 20 min
Cooking : 45-55 min

Ingredients for a tart tin with a diameter of around 28 cm

- *450 g sweet short crust pastry (see recipe page 78)*
- *500 to 600 g cherries*

For the tart custard
- *1 egg*
- *50 g sugar*
- *60 g powdered almonds*
- *50 g crème fraîche*
- *100 g milk*

Butter a 28-cm tart tin.

Roll out the pastry to a thickness of around 2-3 mm and put it into the tart tin.

Prick the bottom with a fork.

Stone the cherries and pour them into the bottom of the tart.

Bake the tart in a preheated oven at 200°C.

For the tart custard

Whisk the egg and the sugar in a salad bowl until light and frothy.

Add the almonds, the cream and the milk and mix.

Pour the custard over your tart after it has been baking for 15 to 20 min.

Put back into the oven for around 30 to 35 min.

When cooked, take the tart out of its tin and put on a rack.

Tarte aux pommes à l'alsacienne
Alsatian-style apple tart or Apfelkuche

Preparation : 20 min
Cooking : 45-55 min

*Ingredients for a tart tin with
a diameter of around 28 cm*

For the short crust pastry
- *250 g flour*
- *125 g butter*
- *30 g caster sugar*
- *4 g salt*
- *1 egg*
- *15 g milk*

For the tart custard
- *1 egg*
- *50 g sugar*
- *100 g crème fraîche*
- *50 g milk*

Other ingredients
- *4 to 6 apples*
- *Butter*

For the short crust pastry

In the bowl of a food mixer or in a salad bowl, mix the flour and the diced butter.

Mix the flour into the butter by rubbing the ingredients vigorously with your hands to obtain a sandy texture.

Incorporate the egg, the milk, the salt and the sugar in the flour and work the pastry until you get a smooth mixture.

Wrap the pastry in Clingfilm and put it in the fridge for an hour.

Preparing the tart custard

Whisk the egg and the sugar in a salad bowl until light and frothy.

Add the milk and cream and mix.

Butter a 28-cm tart tin.

Roll out the pastry to a thickness of around 2-3 mm and put it into the tart tin.

Prick the bottom with a fork.

Peel, core and cut the apples into quarters.

Slice each apple quarter into thin slices.

Arrange them in a rosette on the bottom of the tart.

Bake the tart in a preheated oven at 200°C.

Bake it for around 15 to 20 min and pour the custard over your tart.

Put the tart back into the oven for around 30 to 35 min depending on the oven.

When cooked, take the tart out of its tin and put on a rack.

Tarte aux quetsches à l'alsacienne

Alsatian-style plum tart or Quetschekuche

Preparation : 20 min
Cooking : 45-50 min

Ingredients for a tart tin
with a diameter of around 28 cm

- *450 g short crust pastry*
  (see recipe page 78)
- *800 g dark plums (quetsches)*
- *50 g breadcrumbs*

Other ingredients
- *50 g sugar*
- *½ teaspoon cinnamon*

Butter a 28-cm tart tin.

Roll out the pastry to a thickness of around 3 mm and put it into the tart tin.

Prick the bottom of the tart with a fork.

Sprinkle the breadcrumbs over the bottom of the tart.

Wash and drain the plums, cut them in half, take out the stones and arrange them on the tart.

Arrange them in a rosette on the bottom of the tart.

Bake the tart in a preheated oven at 180°C for around 45 to 50 min.

When cooked, take the tart out of its tin and put on a rack.

Mix the caster sugar and the cinnamon.

Sprinkle the tart with cinnamon sugar.

Tarte flambée aux pommes
Tarte flambée with apples

Preparation : 20 min
Cooking : 8-10 min

Ingredients for three tartes flambées
20 x 30 cm

For the dough
- *250 g flour*
- *5 g salt*
- *150 g water*
- *10 g yeast*
- *20 g butter*

For the fromage blanc mixture
- *150 g fromage blanc*
- *50 g thick cream*
- *50 g sugar*
- *1 egg*

Other ingredients
- *3 to 4 apples*
- *Caster sugar*
- *Powdered cinnamon*
- *1 small glass of Calvados or rum (optional)*
- *Butter*

For the dough

In the food mixer bowl or a salad bowl, mix the flour, the salt, the yeast and the water.

Knead the dough by hand or with the kneading hook in the food mixer.

Put the dough to one side in a salad bowl, cover it with Clingfilm and leave it to double in volume.

For the fromage blanc mixture

Mix the fromage blanc, the egg, the thick cream and the sugar in a bowl.

When the dough has risen sufficiently, turn it out onto a floured work surface.

Cut into the dough into small pieces of around 150 g each.

Flatten the pieces of dough with your hands and then fold the edges into the centre to form a ball.

Roll out the balls to a thickness of around 1 to 2 millimetres.

Place the dough bases on a lightly floured oven tray.

Spread the dough bases with the fromage blanc mixture.

Peel, core and slice the apples and arrange them on the fromage blanc.

Mix the sugar and the cinnamon and sprinkle it over the tartes flambées.

Dot with a few knobs of butter.

Bake in a preheated oven at 260-270°C.

Cooking takes 8 to 10 min depending on your oven.

When you take them out of the oven, drizzle with the Calvados if you wish and flame them.

Serve the tarte flambée immediately while still piping hot.

Tartelettes aux myrtilles
Bilberry tartlets

Preparation : 20 min
Cooking : 30-35 min

*Ingredients for 6 tartlets
around 12 cm in diameter*

• *400 g crumbly short crust pastry
(see recipe page 78)*

Other ingredients
• *400 g bilberries*
• *Butter*
• *Tart custard (see page 18)*

Butter the tartlet tins.

Roll out the pastry to a thickness of around 3 mm.

Cut out discs of pastry 14 cm in diameter and put them in the tartlet tins.

Prick the bottoms with a fork.

Clean, wash and drain the bilberries and arrange them in the tartlet bottoms.

Pour in the tart custard to half way.

Bake in a preheated oven at 180°C for around 30 to 35 min.

When cold, sprinkle the bilberries with caster sugar.

Advice and tips

If using frozen bilberries, sprinkle breadcrumbs sparingly into your tartlet bottoms before adding the bilberries.

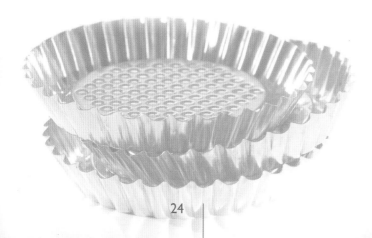

Tarte à la façon de Linz

Tart the way they make it in Linz

Preparation : 20 min
Cooking : 30-40 min

Ingredients for a tart around
20 cm in diameter

• *90 g caster sugar*
• *75 g butter*
• *1 egg*
• *50 g grey powdered almonds*
• *5 g cinnamon*
• *220 g flour*
• *1 g baking powder*

Other ingredients
• *200 g raspberry jam with pips*
• *1 egg for the egg wash glaze*

Sift the flour with the baking powder and the cinnamon.

Cut the butter into small pieces and mix them with the flour.

Rub the flour into the butter and add the grey powdered almonds.

Whisk the sugar and the egg together.

Incorporate the egg in the flour and knead the dough with your hands.

Put the dough in the fridge for at least one hour.

Weigh out around 350 g of dough and roll it out into a circle with a diameter of around 24 cm.

Put the dough in the mould and press it to shape the edges.

Cut off any excess dough with a knife.

Whisk the jam until smooth and spread it over the bottom of the tart.

Roll out the remaining dough to a thickness of 4 mm and cut it into small strips with a fluted cutter.

Criss-cross the strips over the tart.

Brush the criss-crossed strips with the egg wash.

Bake in a preheated oven at 180°C for 30 to 40 min.

Bretzels de carnaval
Carnival bretzels

Preparation : 30 min
Cooking : 8-10 min

Ingredients for 7 to 8 bretzels

- *275 g flour*
- *3 egg yolks*
- *35 g caster sugar*
- *5 g table salt*
- *10 g yeast*
- *25 g milk*
- *80 g water*
- *35 g butter*

Other ingredients
- *1 litre of oil for deep frying*
- *Caster sugar*
- *Cinnamon*

In the bowl of the food mixer, mix the flour, the egg yolks, the milk, the water, the salt, the sugar and the yeast.

Knead the dough with the kneading hook on the food mixer.

When the dough is smooth and shiny, add the softened butter at room temperature.

Mix your dough and when it is evenly mixed, put it to one side in a salad bowl and cover with Clingfilm. Allow the dough to double in volume in a warm place away from draughts.

Turn out the bretzel dough onto a lightly floured work surface.

Cut the dough into pieces of around 70 g each.

Flatten each piece of dough and fold the edges into the centre of your piece of dough until you obtain a small ball.

Shape the balls into sausage shapes.

Stretch the sausage shapes to a length of around 60 cm.

Make a loop with the sausage shapes, cross them and fold over into the middle of the bretzel. Stick down the ends with a little water.

Place the bretzels on a tray covered with a clean cloth.

Cover with Clingfilm and put the tray in a warm place away from draughts.

Heat the oil to 180°C.

As soon as the bretzels have doubled in volume, drop them one by one into the hot oil.

Turn the bretzels over with a wooden spatula. They take 3 to 4 minutes to cook on each side, depending on the size of your bretzels.

When the bretzels are nicely golden, take them out of the oil and drain them on kitchen paper.

Sprinkle with cinnamon sugar while your bretzels are still warm.

Cuisses de dames
Ladies' Thighs or Dameschenkele

Preparation : 25 min
Cooking : 5 min

Ingredients

- 300 g flour
- 5 g baking powder
- 75 g caster sugar
- 75 g butter
- 50 g powdered roast almonds
- 3 eggs

Other ingredients

- Caster sugar
- Powdered cinnamon
- Icing sugar

Mix all the ingredients in the food mixer bowl or in a salad bowl.

Knead the dough by hand or with the kneading hook in the food mixer until evenly mixed.

Roll into a sausage shape around 3 cm in diameter.

Cut slices one cm thick and roll them into small sausage shapes 4 to 5 cm long.

Heat up the oil for deep frying to 180°C.

Carefully drop in a few sausage shapes.

Turn over with a fork after one minute so that they brown nicely.

Let them fry for another minute and then take them out of the deep fat fryer.

Drain them on kitchen paper.

Mix a little caster sugar with the powdered cinnamon.

Roll the thighs in the cinnamon sugar and, if you wish, dust with icing sugar.

Eclats
Chips or Scherwa

Preparation : 15 min
Cooking : 4-5 min

Ingredients

- 500 g flour
- 10 g salt
- 10 g baking powder
- 30 g caster sugar
- 250 g liquid crème fraîche
- 3 eggs
- Grated zest of 1 lemon

Other ingredients

- Caster sugar
- Powdered cinnamon
- Icing sugar

Mix all the ingredients in the food mixer bowl or in a large salad bowl.

Knead the dough by hand or with the kneading hook in the food mixer until evenly mixed.

Spread this dough to a thickness of around 5 mm.

Using a fluted roller, cut out lozenges around 4 cm square.

Heat the deep fat fryer to 180°C.

Carefully drop in a few lozenges of dough.

After one minute, turn them over with a fork so that they brown evenly on both sides.

Let them fry for another minute and then take them out of the deep fat fryer.

Drain them on kitchen paper.

Roll the chips in caster sugar or cinnamon sugar and, if you wish, dust with icing sugar.

Agneau Pascal
Easter Lamb or Lamele

Preparation : 30 min
Cooking : 40-45 min

Ingredients for 1 mould

- 4 egg whites
- 60 g sugar + 60 g sugar
- 4 egg yolks
- 20 g corn flour
- 100 g flour
- Zest of 1 lemon

Other ingredients

- 50 g butter
- Flour

Preheat your oven to 180°C.

Liberally butter and flour your earthenware lamb mould.

Remove any excess flour, assemble the mould and place it on an oven tray.

Sift the flour with the corn flour.

In a bowl, whisk the egg yolks and the sugar to a foam.

Beat the egg whites as if making a meringue with the rest of the sugar.

When the egg whites form stiff peaks, add and mix in the yolks and then gently fold in the flour and the lemon zest with a spatula.

Do not over mix the preparation in order to keep the air in it.

Pour the biscuit mix into the mould and bake for around 40 to 45 min depending on your oven.

Check that it is cooked with the point of a small knife: if the blade comes out dry, your lamb is cooked.

After it is cooked and completely cold, dust generously with icing sugar.

Decorate with a ribbon or a small flag.

Tips

Just like for the Kougelhopf, it is better to use an earthenware mould which will impart its very specific flavour much better.

When using your mould for the first time, butter it liberally and bake in the oven for a good hour. Allow to cool down until the next day and then clean it with kitchen paper but do not wash it.

Bonhomme de Saint Nicolas
Saint Nicholas Figure or Manele

Preparation : 25 min
Cooking : 15 min

In the food mixer bowl or a large salad bowl, mix the flour, the sugar, the salt, the yeast, the egg and the milk.

Knead the dough by hand or with the kneading hook in the food mixer.

When the dough is smooth, add the softened butter.

Mix the dough until it is again smooth and evenly mixed.

Cover the dough with Clingfilm and allow it to double in volume in a warm place away from draughts.

When the dough has risen sufficiently, turn it out onto a floured work surface.

Cut into the dough into small pieces of around 75g each.

Flatten each piece of dough with your hand and then fold over the edges of the dough into the centre to form a ball. Stretch out the balls and form small, carrot-shaped dough sausages.

Take the widest part and shape the figure's head with the side of your hand.

Place the pieces of dough on a buttered oven tray.

Press the figures onto the oven tray and, with a small knife, make cuts into the body to form the arms.

Then cut the bottom part into two equal parts for the legs.

Ingredients for around 8 figures

- 300 g fine wheat flour
- 50 g caster sugar
- 5 g table salt
- 1 egg
- 20 g yeast
- 110 g milk
- 75 g butter

Other ingredients

- 1 egg for the egg wash glaze
- Raisins or chocolate chips

Press two raisins into each figure for the eyes and one for the belly button.

Cover the figures with Clingfilm and allow them to double in volume in a warm place away from draughts.

When the dough has doubled in volume, brush with the egg wash.

Bake in an oven preheated to 180°C for around 15 min.

Brioche de Noël
Christmas Brioche or Christollen

Preparation : 35 min
Cooking : 30 min

Place the hazelnuts, the walnuts and the chopped almonds on an oven tray.

Roast in the oven at a temperature of 160°C until slightly browned.

In the food mixer bowl or a salad bowl, mix the flour, the egg, the milk, the salt, the sugar and the yeast.

Knead the dough by hand or with the kneading hook in the food mixer. When the dough is smooth, add the softened butter.

Mix your dough again until the butter is incorporated and the dough smooth.

Add the cold roasted nuts, the diced orange and lemon peel, the raisins macerated in rum and the grated lemon zest and mix thoroughly.

Cover the dough with Clingfilm and allow it to double in volume in a warm place away from draughts.

When the dough has doubled in volume, turn it out onto a lightly floured work surface.

Divide the dough in two, shape the pieces into balls and allow to rest for 15 min.

With a rolling pin, roll out the balls to obtain oval discs around 25 cm long and 15 cm wide.

Fold in two over the almond paste and place the Christmas brioches on a buttered oven tray.

Brush the brioches with the melted butter and leave to rise in a warm place.

When the dough has doubled in volume, brush again with the butter and bake in a preheated oven at 180°C. Cooking takes around 30 min.

When cooked, brush one last time with melted butter and, depending on your taste, sprinkle with cinnamon sugar or sift icing sugar over the Christmas brioches.

Ingredients

- 250 g flour
- 5 g salt
- 40 g caster sugar
- 15 g yeast
- 1 egg
- 80 g milk
- 75 g butter
- 25 g raisins macerated in rum
- 50 g diced candied orange peel
- 50 g diced candied lemon peel
- 50 g whole hazelnuts
- 50 g chopped almonds
- 25 g chopped walnuts
- Grated zest of ½ a lemon

Other ingredients

- 50 g melted butter for brushing
- 150 g unflavoured almond paste
- Cinnamon sugar or icing sugar

Cœurs de pain d'épices
Gingerbread Hearts

Preparation : 25 min
Cooking : 15-20 min

Ingredients for 2 or 3 hearts

- *350 g flour*
- *200 g honey*
- *60 g sugar*
- *1 egg*
- *1 egg yolk*
- *6 g baking powder*
- *5 g milk*
- *5 g kirsch*
- *5 g cinnamon*
- *6 g gingerbread spices*

Other ingredients
- *Milk*
- *Whole almonds, glacé cherries, star anise, cinnamon stick, walnut kernels, hazelnuts, almonds, cardamom seeds, pistachios…*

The day before

Mix the flour, the cinnamon and the gingerbread spices.

Mix the milk with the baking powder.

Put the honey and the sugar in a saucepan and warm over a low heat.

When the honey is warm (around 60°C), pour it into the flour and knead the dough.

Incorporate the eggs and knead until completely cold.

Then add the kirsch and the baking powder mixed with milk.

Wrap the dough in Clingfilm and keep it in the fridge for at least 24 hours.

On the day

Take the dough out of the fridge one hour before use.

Roll out a small piece of dough and do a baking test in a preheated oven at 180°C: if the top of the dough is blistered, rework it with a little flour to firm it up.

Roll out the dough to a thickness of 5 mm.

Cut out the hearts with a heart-shaped cutter.

Place the hearts on a lightly floured oven tray.

Brush the hearts with cold milk.

Decorate with the fruits and spices.

Bake in a preheated oven at 180°C for 15 to 20 min.

Allow the hearts to cool down before wrapping them.

Langues de pain d'épices

Gingerbread tongues or LebkucheZunge

Preparation : 35 min
Cooking : 8-10 min

Ingredients

For the gingerbread dough
- 300 g flour
- 200 g honey
- 60 g caster sugar
- 1 egg yolk
- 1 egg
- 6 g baking powder
- 2 tbsp milk
- 5 g kirsch
- 5 g cinnamon
- 6 g gingerbread spices
- 50 g toasted chopped almonds
- 50 g toasted chopped hazelnuts
- 50 g diced candied lemon peel
- 50 g diced candied orange peel

For the royal icing
- 1 egg white
- 150 g sifted icing sugar

Other ingredients
- Milk

The day before

In the food mixer bowl or a large bowl, mix the flour, the cinnamon and the gingerbread spices.

In another bowl, mix the milk and the baking powder.

Put the honey and the sugar in a saucepan and warm over a low heat.

When the honey reaches approximately 60°C, pour it on to the flour and knead the dough with a wooden spatula or the kneading hook on the food mixer.

Incorporate the eggs while continuing to mix the dough.

Knead the dough until it is completely cold.

Then add the kirsch and the baking powder mixed with milk.

Finish the preparation by incorporating the nuts and the candied peel.

Wrap the dough in Clingfilm and put in the fridge.

On the day

Take your dough out of the fridge and allow it to come to room temperature for thirty minutes.

On a lightly floured work surface, roll out the dough to a thickness of 1 to 2 mm.

Remove any surplus flour and cut out the tongues using a gingerbread cutter.

Place the tongues on a lightly floured oven tray. Brush the tongues with cold milk. Bake straight away in a preheated oven at 180°C for 8 to 10 min. After baking, let your gingerbread tongues cool before removing them from the oven tray.

Whisk the egg white and the icing sugar together. When the royal icing is thoroughly mixed, brush over the tongues. Let the icing dry in the oven for 1 to 2 min at 160°C.

Pain aux fruits
Fruit loaf or Hutzelbrot

Preparation : 40 min
Cooking : 45-50 min

The day before

Cut the fruits and nuts into small cubes of the same size and mix them with the sugar, the honey and the alcohol. Put it all into an airtight container.

The next day

In the food mixer bowl or a large salad bowl, mix the flour, the yeast, the salt and the milk.

Knead the dough by hand or with the kneading hook in the food mixer until smooth and evenly mixed.

Cover the dough with Clingfilm and allow it to double in volume in a warm place away from draughts.

Gradually incorporate the macerated fruits into the dough by hand.

When mixing is finished, the dough is completely bound to the fruits.

Weigh out pieces of 300 g each.

Moisten the work surface and your hands to shape the pieces of dough into elongated loaves.

Put them straight on to an oven tray covered with greaseproof paper.

Decorate with the halved glacé cherries and the walnut kernels.

Leave to rest for half an hour and baked in a preheated oven at 160-170°C for 45 to 50 min.

Mix the sugar and the water in a saucepan and bring to a rolling boil. Brush the fruit loaves with the hot syrup as soon as you take them out of the oven.

Ingredients for 2 loaves

For the fruit mix
- *50 g dried dates*
- *50 g dried figs*
- *50 g dried apples*
- *50 g dried pears*
- *40 g dried apricots*
- *60 g walnuts*
- *40 g prunes*
- *30 g raisins*
- *25 g caster sugar*
- *25 g honey*
- *60 g Alsatian kirsch*

For the dough
- *5 g yeast*
- *80 g flour*
- *2 g salt*
- *50 g milk*

For the syrup
- *30 g water*
- *50 g sugar*

Other ingredients
- *Glacé cherries*
- *Walnut kernels*

Advice and special tips

Check the temperature using a metal needle:

stick the needle into the fruit loaf, wait 5 seconds, take it out again and if the needle is hot to the touch, your fruit loaf is cooked.

Brioches de Nouvel An
New Year Brioches or Stollen

Preparation : 25 min
Cooking : 15-20 min

Ingredients for 8 brioches

- 250 g flour
- 40 g caster sugar
- 5 g table salt
- 2 eggs
- 10 g yeast
- 40 g milk
- 65 g butter
- 60 g currants

Other ingredients

- 1 egg for the egg wash glaze

Tips

In order to stop the scissors sticking to the dough, dip the points of the scissors in the egg wash before cutting the Stollen.

In the food mixer bowl or a large salad bowl, mix the flour, the eggs, the milk, the salt, the sugar and the yeast.

Knead the dough by hand or with the kneading hook in the food mixer.

When the dough is smooth and shiny, add the softened butter at room temperature.

Mix your dough and, when it is evenly mixed, gently incorporate the currants.

Cover the dough with Clingfilm and allow to double in volume in a warm place.

Turn out the Stollen dough onto a lightly floured work surface.

Weigh out pieces of 70g each.

Flatten the pieces of dough and fold the edges into the centre of your piece of dough until you obtain nice round balls of smooth dough.

Place the balls of dough on a buttered oven tray.

Allow the Stollen rise in a warm place away from draughts.

When they have doubled in volume, brush with the egg wash.

Make four cuts in each piece of dough with a pair of scissors. The scissor cuts should form a cross.

Bake the Stollen in a preheated oven at 180°C.

Cooking takes around 15 to 20 min depending on your oven.

Forêt-Noire

Black Forest Gateau or Schwartzwalder

Preparation : 45 min
Cooking : 10 min

Recipe for 6 servings

Ingredients for the chocolate sponge
- *4 eggs*
- *120 g sugar*
- *100 g flour*
- *30 g cocoa powder*

Syrup
- *100 g water*
- *100 g sugar*
- *50 g kirsch*

Whipped cream
- *500 g liquid crème fraîche*
- *50 g caster sugar*

Other ingredients
- *400 g morello cherries*
- *1 bar of dark chocolate*

For the chocolate sponge

Warm the eggs and the sugar in a bain-marie to around 50°C.

Then beat the eggs with an electric whisk until you obtain a light froth.

Sift the flour and the cocoa powder and then, with a spatula, carefully incorporate the flour into the first mixture. Try not to let the mixture collapse by mixing too long.

Divide and spread this mixture on two oven trays covered with greaseproof paper using a palette knife to a thickness of around 8 mm. Bake in a preheated oven at 220°C for around 10 min.

When you take it out of the oven, slide the sponge disc on to the work surface.

For the syrup

Bring the water and the sugar to the boil to make a syrup and let it cool down. Add the kirsch.

For the whipped cream

Beat the well chilled cream and the sugar with an electric whisk or a hand whisk to obtain an unctuous whipped cream.

Assembling the Black Forest Gateau

Prepare the whipped cream and put it into a piping bag fitted with a straight 10-mm nozzle. With a cutter 10 cm in diameter, cut out 18 discs of chocolate sponge.

Brush with the syrup.

Cover six sponge bases with whipped cream to obtain a layer one centimetre thick.

Scatter with morello cherries in syrup.

Position the second layer of sponge and repeat.

Position the top layer of sponge and cover with whipped cream.

Grate a bar of chocolate with a vegetable peeler to make shavings.

Sprinkle each Black Forest Gateau with chocolate shavings.

Keep in the fridge until ready to serve.

Granité aux quetsches
Plum crumble or Gremmelkueche

Preparation : 15 min
Cooking : 45 min

Ingredients for the crumble

- 250 g flour
- 5 g baking powder
- 5 g cinnamon
- 100 g caster sugar
- 75 g butter
- 1 egg

Other ingredients
- 600 g Alsatian plums (quetsches)
- Icing sugar
- Butter

Rub the flour, the baking powder, the cinnamon and the butter with your hands until the mixture takes on a sandy appearance.

Mix the egg and the sugar and incorporate this mixture into the sandy preparation.

Work the preparation with your fingertips in order to obtain little lumps.

When the crumble has been mixed, put it in the fridge for around one hour.

Stone the plums.

Prepare a buttered baking dish and spread more than half of the crumble in the bottom.

Arrange the plums on the crumble in closely packed rows.

Cover the plums with the remaining crumble.

Bake in a preheated oven at 200°C for around 40 to 45 min.

Serving

This dessert can be eaten hot, warm or cold.

Mendiant

Mendiant or Bettelman

Preparation : 20 min
Cooking : 35-45 min

Ingredients

- 200 g stale bread or sandwich loaf
- 150 g caster sugar
- 2 eggs
- 400 g milk

- 600 g cherries

Other ingredients
- Butter
- Breadcrumbs

I to 2 hours in advance

Break up the bread and put it in a large salad bowl.

Boil the milk, pour it on to the bread and mix together for one minute.

When the sandwich loaf is thoroughly soft, add the sugar and the eggs.

Mix the ingredients with a spatula until evenly mixed.

Correct the consistency with a little milk if necessary.

The mixture should have the same texture as mashed potato.

Stem the cherries and incorporate them in the mixture.

Mix gently with a spatula.

Liberally butter an oven dish or individual ramekins.

Pour the preparation into the mould.

Sprinkle with the breadcrumbs.

Bake in a preheated oven at 180°C for around 35 to 45 min.

Let the mendiant cool down in the dish.

Nid d'abeille

Honeycomb

Preparation : I hour
Cooking : 30-35 min

Ingredients for I 24-cm tart tin

For the dough
- *I50 g flour*
- *3 g table salt*
- *30 g caster sugar*
- *I0 g yeast*
- *I egg*
- *30 g milk*
- *50 g butter*

For the honeycomb mix
- *30 g butter*
- *30 g caster sugar*
- *20 g honey*
- *I0 g milk*
- *50 g flaked almonds*

Other ingredients
- *Confectioner's custard*
  (see p. 79)
- *I egg for the egg wash glaze*
- *Butter*
- *Rum*

For the dough

In the food mixer bowl with the kneading hook, mix and knead the flour, the sugar, the salt, the yeast, the egg and the milk. When the dough is smooth, add the softened butter. Mix the dough thoroughly.

Cover the dough and leave to double in volume. When the dough has risen sufficiently, turn it out onto a floured work surface.

Flatten it with your hands and then fold the edges into the centre to form a ball.

Turn over the ball of dough and roll it out to the size of a 24-cm tart tin.

Put the dough in the buttered tin.

Let the dough double in volume in the tin.

For the honeycomb mix

Put the butter, the sugar, the milk and the honey in a saucepan. Heat the mixture until the sugar dissolves. Add the flaked almonds and mix. Pour the mix onto the dough while still hot.

Construction

When the dough has doubled in volume, brush with the egg wash.

Spread the mix evenly with the flaked almonds over the entire surface using a palette knife.

Bake in a preheated oven at I80°C. It will take around 30 to 35 min to cook.

When cooked, take the honeycomb out of the tart tin and put it on a rack until completely cooled.

Whisk the confectioner's custard with the rum. Slice the honeycomb horizontally with a serrated knife. With a palette knife, spread the custard on the bottom of the honeycomb.

Put the top back on with the almonds on the confectioner's custard and keep the honeycomb in the fridge.

Savarin au Kirsch d'Alsace

et coulis de griottes Savarin with Alsatian kirsch and morello cherry coulis

Preparation : 40 min
Cooking : 20 min

Ingredients for 6 savarins with kirsch

For the dough
- *75 g flour*
- *12 g caster sugar*
- *1 g table salt*
- *2 eggs*
- *5 g yeast*
- *20 g butter*

For the morello cherry coulis
- *200 g morello cherries in syrup, drained*
- *100 g caster sugar*

For the syrup
- *500 g water*
- *250 g sugar*

Other ingredients and equipment
- *6 small, individual Kougelhopf moulds in silicone*
- *100 g liquid cream for the whipped cream*
- *6 morello cherries in kirsch*
- *1 small glass of kirsch*

For the savarin dough

In a salad bowl or the food mixer bowl, mix the flour, the sugar, the salt, the yeast and the eggs. Melt the butter and add it to the mixture.

When evenly mixed, put the soft dough into a piping bag fitted with a straight nozzle of around 10 mm.

Fill the Kougelhopf moulds to a third of their height.

Let the savarins rise to the top of the moulds and bake at 180°C for around 20 min.

Take out of the moulds and leave the little Kougelhopfs to cool on a rack.

For the morello cherry coulis

Blend the morello cherries and the sugar and strain the resulting pulp through a sieve.

Put the coulis in the fridge until ready to use.

For the soaking syrup

Prepare a syrup with 500 g of water and 250 g of sugar. Boil and leave to cool to around 50°C.

Assembly

Soak the Kougelhopfs head first for 2 min and then turn them over and leave them to soak for a further 5 min.

Take them out with a slotted spoon and leave them to drain on a rack.

Drizzle some morello cherry coulis on to each plate.

Drizzle the savarins with a spoonful of kirsch and put them on the plates.

Garnish each savarin with a rosette of whipped cream and decorate with a morello cherry macerated in kirsch.

Serve chilled.

Tarte biscuitée au Kirsch
Biscuit-based tart with Kirsch

Preparation : 1 hour
Cooking : 35-40 min

Ingredients for 9 small tarts
8 cm in diameter

For the tart bases
- *60 g egg white*
- *60 g sugar*
- *20 g powdered hazelnuts*
- *20 g powdered almonds*
- *10 g flour*

For the biscuit dough
(See p. 79)

For the syrup
- *100 g water*
- *75 g sugar*
- *15 g kirsch*

For the buttered cream
- *150 g sugar*
- *50 g water*
- *1 egg*
- *200 g butter*
- *20 g kirsch*

For the tart bases

Mix the powdered hazelnuts and almonds with the flour. Beat the egg whites with the sugar as if you were making a supple meringue. Gently incorporate the flour, hazelnut and almond mixture with a spatula.

Fill a piping bag fitted with an 8-mm nozzle. Using the piping bag, dispose the tart base dough in spirals to make 9 discs 8 cm in diameter.

Bake for around 25 min at 160°C.

For the syrup

Boil, allow to cool and add the Kirsch.

For the buttered cream

Bring the sugar and the water up to a temperature of 118°C.

Gradually pour the hot sugar syrup on to the egg while whisking. Whip the mixture to a foam in the mixer and add the butter while it is still warm. Whip the cream to an emulsion for around 10 min in the mixer and add the kirsch.

Assembly

Cut out the tart bases (save any crumbs) and the biscuits with a cutter.

Spread a 2-mm layer of buttered cream on to the tart bases with a spatula. Put a biscuit base on the cream and brush it with syrup. Spread the biscuit bases with a layer of buttered cream 4 mm thick. Add the final biscuit bases and brush with the remaining syrup. Crush any crumbs from the tart bases with a rolling pin.

Spread a fine layer of buttered cream around the edge of the biscuits and roll them in the tart base crumbs (which can be replaced by toasted powdered hazelnuts). Spread the top of each tart with a fine layer of buttered cream and dust with icing sugar.

Score with a knife to decorate and keep in the fridge until ready to serve.

Torche aux marrons
Chestnut cream tartlets

Preparation : 40 min
Cooking : 25 min

Ingredients for 6 tartlets

• *450 g sweet pastry*
(see p. 79)

For the whipped cream

• *150 g crème fraîche*

• *15 g caster sugar*

• *Chestnut cream*

• *200 g tin unsweetened chestnut purée*

• *250 g tin sweetened chestnut cream*

• *75 g butter*

• *1 tbsp rum*

Other ingredients

• *6 plain meringues*

Roll out the dough to a thickness of 2 mm with a rolling pin and put into individual tartlet moulds.

Place greaseproof paper over the dough and fill the moulds with baking beans.

Bake for 25 min at 180°C.

Carefully remove the paper and the baking beans from the tart moulds and leave to cool.

For the chestnut cream

Blend the chestnut purée, the chestnut cream, the butter and the rum in a mixer.

For the whipped cream

Whip the well chilled crème fraîche and the sugar to obtain an unctuous whipped cream.

Fill a piping bag fitted with a fluted 10-mm nozzle with the whipped cream.

Spread a layer of whipped cream in the tartlet bases.

Break the meringues into large pieces and scatter them on the cream and cover with whipped cream.

Fill a piping bag fitted with a 2-3-mm nozzle with the chestnut mixture.

Cover the tartlets with chestnut vermicelli.

Keep in the fridge until ready to serve.

Demi-lunes
Half-moons or Kipfers

Preparation : 20 min
Cooking : 15 min

Ingredients

- *250 g flour*
- *200 g butter*
- *80 g caster sugar*
- *1 sachet of vanilla sugar*
- *2 egg yolks*
- *100 g powdered almonds*

Other ingredients

- *Icing sugar*

Break the eggs and separate the yolks from the whites.

In a salad bowl, whisk the egg yolks with the sugar and the vanilla sugar.

In a different bowl, rub the butter into the flour until you obtain a sandy-looking mass.

This is done by rubbing the flour and the butter with your fingertips.

Incorporate the almonds and the sweetened egg yolk mixture with the flour and mix to obtain an evenly mixed dough.

Wrap the dough in Clingfilm and put it in the fridge for around an hour.

Gently work the dough and make sausage shapes around 3 cm in diameter.

Cut the large pieces into 1-cm sections in order to ensure more or less the same weight for each biscuit.

Stretch these small pieces of dough and shape them into half-moons.

Put them on an oven tray which you have buttered or covered with greaseproof paper.

Bake in a preheated oven at 180°C for around 15 min.

Sprinkle with icing sugar immediately after baking.

These little biscuits can easily be kept for several weeks in an airtight biscuit tin stored in a cool dry place.

Etoiles à la cannelle
Cinnamon stars or Zimmetsterne

Preparation : 30 min
Cooking : 10 min

Ingredients for around 570 g
of dough

• *250 g icing sugar*
• *5 g cinnamon*
• *250 g powdered whole almonds*
• *70 g egg whites or 2 egg whites*

Other ingredients
• *1 egg white*
• *150 g icing sugar*

Sift the icing sugar with the cinnamon into a salad bowl.

Add the powdered almonds and the egg whites.

Work the mixture to obtain a smooth dough.

When the dough has been sufficiently kneaded, wrap it in Clingfilm and put it in the fridge for around an hour.

Gently knead the dough on the work surface and roll it out to a thickness of around 10 mm.

Keep the dough in the fridge or even in the freezer for 15 min.

Put the egg white and the icing sugar in a bowl.

Whisk the egg white and the icing sugar to obtain a quite firm royal icing.

Using a spoon, spread a fine layer of royal icing on the dough.

Soak the cinnamon start cutter in a bowl of water and cut out stars from the dough.

Place them on an oven tray covered with greaseproof paper or a silicone baking mat.

Rework any remaining dough with a little powdered almond and repeat the operations described above.

Leave the stars to dry out for around 2 hours at room temperature.

Bake in a preheated oven at 170°C for around 10 min.

When the stars are cold, put them in an airtight tin and store in a cool, dry place.

Macarons à la noix de coco

Coconut macaroons or Kokosmakrenle

Preparation : 20 min
Kochzeit : 12 min

Ingredients for around 600 g of macaroons

- 160g egg whites or approx. 5 egg whites
- 225 g caster sugar
- 225 g grated coconut
- ½ vanilla pod

Put the egg white and the sugar in a saucepan.

Heat the preparation, whisking it all the time.

At approximately 50°C, add the grated coconut and the scraped vanilla with a wooden spatula.

Work the mixture until evenly mixed and leave to cool.

Fill a piping bag fitted with a fluted nozzle around 14 mm in diameter with the macaroon dough.

Pipe rosettes on to an oven tray which you have buttered or covered with greaseproof paper.

Bake in a preheated oven at 180°C for around 12 min.

Advice and tips

If the macaroon dough is too stiff, add a little egg white to obtain the correct consistency.

You can ring the changes by adding chocolate chips and a little rum.

Baking must be very brief. The outside should be crisp while the inside remains chewy.

Petits fours à l'anis
Anise-flavoured petits fours or Anisbredle

Preparation : 25 min
Cooking : 10 min

Ingredients for around 400 g of anise-flavoured petits fours

- 2 eggs
- 165 g caster sugar
- 170 g wheat flour
- 8 g anise seeds

Other ingredients

- Butter
- Flour

Break the eggs into a saucepan and add the sugar.

Heat and whisk until the mixture reaches a temperature of around 50°C. Pour this mixture into the bowl of an electric mixer.

Beat for around 10 min or until the mixture doubles in volume.

Sift the flour and, using a wooden spatula, incorporate it with the anise seeds into the beaten eggs.

Put the dough into a piping bag fitted with a straight nozzle around 10 mm in diameter.

Pipe small discs on to a very lightly buttered and floured oven tray.

Leave the petits fours to form a crust in a dry place for around 2 hours or until the crust is thick enough; it should crack when pressed with a finger.

Preheat a conventionally heated oven to 180°C and then put the oven tray into the oven.

Bake for around 10 min or until browned sufficiently.

Petits-beurre
Butter biscuits or Butterbredele

Preparation : 20 min
Cooking : 10-15 min

Ingredients for 580 g of dough

- 250 g flour
- 3 g baking powder
- 150 g butter
- 125 g icing sugar
- 1 egg
- ½ scraped vanilla pod
- 1 pinch of salt

Other ingredients
- 1 egg for the egg wash glaze

Break the egg into a salad bowl and add the sugar.

Incorporate the scraped vanilla and the pinch of salt and whisk together immediately.

Sift the flour with the baking powder.

Mix the flour and the butter to obtain a sandy-looking mixture.

This is done by rubbing the flour and the butter between your hands.

Incorporate the egg and sugar mixture with the sandy flour and work the dough to obtain an even mixture.

When the dough has been kneaded, wrap it in Clingfilm.

Put in the fridge for around two hours.

Gently knead the dough and roll it out to a thickness of around 4 mm.

Cut into various shapes using biscuit cutters.

Put the butter biscuits on an oven tray which you have lightly buttered or covered with greaseproof paper.

Brush them with the egg wash.

Leave to dry and brush with the egg wash a second time.

Bake in a preheated oven at 180°C for around 10 to 15 min.

Rochers aux noix
Walnut rock meringues

Preparation : 25 min
Cooking : 1 to 1¼ hours

Ingredients

- 120 g egg whites
(around 4 egg whites)
- 240 g caster sugar
- 300 g walnuts

Put the egg whites and the sugar in a saucepan.

Heat and whisk until the egg whites reach a temperature of around 60°C.

Pour this mixture in the bowl of an electric mixer.

Beat for around 10 minutes to obtain a firm meringue.

Incorporate the walnuts with a wooden spatula.

Using a small spoon, put small rocks on to an oven tray covered with greaseproof paper or a silicone baking mat.

Bake in a preheated oven at 110°C for around 1 to 1¼ hours.

Advice and special tips

These little meringues can easily be kept for several weeks in an airtight biscuit tin in a cool dry place.

Sablés souabes
Swabian shortbread or Schwowebredele

Preparation : 20 min
Cooking : 10-15 min

Ingredients for 700 g of dough

* 250 g flour
* 3 g baking powder
* 175 g butter
* 125 g caster sugar
* 1 egg
* 50 g powdered almonds
* 50 g powdered hazelnuts
* 5 g cinnamon
* 1 pinch of salt

Other ingredients
* 1 egg for the egg wash glaze

Break the egg into a salad bowl, add the sugar and the pinch of salt and whisk together.

Sift the flour with the baking powder.

Mix the flour and the butter until you obtain a sandy-looking mixture.

This is done by rubbing the flour and the butter with your fingertips.

Incorporate the almonds, the hazelnuts, the cinnamon and the egg and sugar mixture with the sandy flour and work the dough to obtain an even mixture.

When the dough has been sufficiently kneaded, wrap it in Clingfilm and put it in the fridge for around an hour.

Roll out the dough to a thickness of around 3 to 4 mm.

Cut out various shapes with biscuit cutters.

Put the shortbreads on an oven tray which you have lightly buttered or covered with greaseproof paper.

Brush with the egg wash.

Leave to dry and brush with the egg wash a second time.

If you wish, decorate with nuts, candied fruits or sugar.

Bake in a preheated oven at 180°C for around 10 to 15 min.

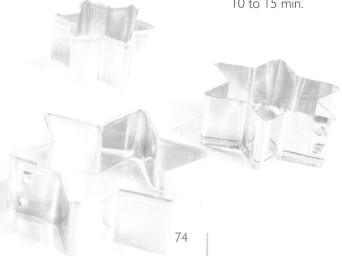

Spritzbredle
Spritzbredele

Preparation : 20 min
Cooking : 10-15 min

---

*Ingredients for around 500 g
of Spritzbredele*

- *250 g flour*
- *3 g baking powder*
- *150 g butter*
- *150 g caster sugar*
- *1 egg*
- *35 g powdered almonds*
- *40 g powdered hazelnuts*

Break the egg into a salad bowl and add the sugar.

Whisk straight away.

Sift the flour with the baking powder.

Mix the flour and the butter until you obtain a sandy-looking mixture.

This job can be done with a food processor or on the work surface by rubbing the flour and butter with your hands.

Incorporate the egg and the sugar and the powdered hazelnuts and almonds into the sandy flour and work the dough until evenly mixed.

Wrap the dough in Clingfilm and put it in the fridge for around an hour.

Lightly knead the dough.

Have a mincer ready fitted with a star-shaped fitting to shape the Spritzbredele.

Turn on the mincer and cut off small sections, which you then place on an oven tray that you have buttered or covered with greaseproof paper.

Shape into laces, crowns or batons.

Bake them in a preheated oven at 170°C for around 10 to 15 min.

La pâte brisée Short crust pastry

Preparation : 20 min

Ingredients for a tart tin with a diameter of around 28 cm

- 250 g flour
- 125 g butter
- 30 g caster sugar
- 4 g salt
- 1 egg
- 15 g milk

In the bowl of a food mixer or in a salad bowl, mix the flour and the diced butter.

Mix the flour into the butter by rubbing the ingredients vigorously with your hands to obtain a sandy texture.

Incorporate the egg, the milk, the salt and the sugar in the flour and work the pastry until you get a smooth mixture.

Wrap the pastry in Clingfilm and put it in the fridge for an hour before using.

La pâte sablée Crumbly short crust pastry

Preparation : 20 min

Ingredients for a tart tin with a diameter of around 28 cm

- 250 g flour
- 1 pinch of baking powder
- 1 pinch of salt
- 150 g butter
- 150 g caster sugar
- 1 egg

Sift the flour and the baking powder into a salad bowl.

Mix the flour with the butter and salt and rub the mixture between your hands to obtain a sandy-looking mix.

Whisk the egg and the sugar in a salad bowl.

Incorporate the egg with the flour and knead the pastry to obtain a smooth mixture.

When the pastry is kneaded, put it in the fridge for around an hour before using.

La pâte à biscuit Biscuit dough

Preparation : 30 min
Cooking : 7 min

Ingredients

- 3 egg whites
- 90 g sugar
- 3 beaten egg yolks
- 75 g flour
- 20 g starch

Mix the flour with the starch.

Beat the egg whites and the sugar as if you were making a firm but supple meringue.

Add and mix the yolks with a spatula and then gently incorporate the sifted flour.

Fill a piping bag fitted with an 8-mm nozzle.

Using the piping bag, dispose the biscuit dough in spirals to make 18 disks 8 cm in diameter.

Bake for around 7 min at 200°C.

La crème pâtissière Confectioner's custard

Preparation : 20 min
Cooking : 5 min

Ingredients

- 200 g milk
- 40 g caster sugar
- 20 g confectioner's custard powder
- 2 egg yolks
- 40 g butter

Whisk the custard powder and half of the sugar together in a bowl.

Put the milk and the butter in a saucepan with the rest of the sugar and heat.

Whisk the egg yolks with the sugar and custard powder mix.

When the milk starts to boil, pour some of the hot milk onto the egg mixture and whisk vigorously. Then pour the cooler mixture into the boiling milk and bring the confectioner's custard to the boil, stirring all the time. As soon as the custard starts to bubble, pour it into a salad bowl, cover it with Clingfilm and keep in the fridge.

Remerciements :

Les auteurs tiennent à remercier toutes les personnes, qui de près
ou de loin, nous ont permis la réalisation de cet ouvrage et nous ont apporté leur aide.

Un remerciement tout particulier à
Sandrine, Martine, Frédérique, Marie, Bernard, Damien et Antoine.

Auteurs
Gérard Fritsch et Guy Zeissloff

Photographe
Frédérique Clément
www.fredclement.com

Maquette
I.D. Créations, Damien Schitter

Relecture
Marie Heckmann et Antoine Dounovetz

I.D. l'Édition
9, rue des Artisans - 67210 Bernardswiller
Tél. : 03 88 34 22 00 - Fax : 03 88 34 26 26
id.edition@wanadoo.fr - www.id-edition.com

ISBN : 978-2-915626-96-4
Impression : EU
octobre 2013